SIGNAL BOOKS SIGNATURE POETS SERIES

THE BODY'S HORIZON

Kathryn Kirkpatrick

THE AUTHOR

Kathryn Kirkpatrick lives in Vilas, North Carolina, and is Associate Professor of English at Appalachian State University. She holds a Ph.D. in Interdisciplinary Studies from Emory University, where she also received an Academy of American Poets poetry prize.

Library of Congress Cataloging-in-Publication Data

Kirkpatrick, Kathryn J.
    Body's Horizon: poems / by Kathryn Kirkpatrick.
        p.   cm.
    ISBN 0-930095-03-0 (alk. paper)
    I. Title.
PS3561.I7125B63   1995
811'.54—dc20   95-26841
                                          CIP

For Billy

ACKNOWLEDGMENTS

Grateful acknowledgment is made to the following publications, in which these poems first appeared:

Birmingham Poetry Review: "Magdalene"; *Cold Mountain Review*: "Año Nuevo"; *Epoch*: "Groping for Trout"; *Gulf Stream*: "Living Together," "On Laundry"; *Kennesaw Review*: "Dreams of Departure," "A Poet Explains Deconstruction"; *Poem*: "Nobel Physicist Creates Theory From Geologist Son's Data," "For My Father, Who Never Sang," "Sacrament of Sleep," "Corrida," "The Daughter," "Flight," "Temperance," "Reliving the Myths," "Sycamore," "Shark's Teeth"; *Shenandoah*: "Sigune to Parzival: Discourse on Grief"; *South Carolina Review*: "The Traveler," "Britomart Writes from Malecasta's Castle"; *Southern Poetry Review*: "When the Bleeding Comes"; *Sow's Ear Poetry Journal*: "The Pledge"; *Sycamore Review*: "Good Friday in Logroño," "What I Knew"; *Telescope*: "To Fear Death By Water"; *Willow Review*: "El Mercado."

I want to thank Susan Ludvigson for her help with these poems, for her loving support over many years of writing and friendship, and for the joyful example she sets. I am also grateful to Bob Hill for his careful attention to this manuscript, and for his unwavering generosity and encouragement.

CONTENTS

1. THE DAUGHTER

2. KEEPING THE FEAST

3. WINDOW ON SPAIN

4. LIVING TOGETHER

1. THE DAUGHTER

FOR MY FATHER, WHO NEVER SANG

Ahead of me in line
a man sorts through groceries
he can't afford:
he picks out two cans of pork and beans,
one in each hand,
and stands for a moment, deciding.
I'm in no hurry, but the register clerk
glowers, each discard building his grudge,
his anger scrolling like the long white tape
of prices he must re-add. He looks at me, and I know
what he's asking. He wants me to second his fury.
We are to conspire, his set jaw seems to say,
against the folly of mismanaged budgets,
against those absurd little hopes that land
like miscalculated jumps of young grasshoppers,
just outside our means. He is waiting
as the man decides to keep
his Sara Lee creme-filled sandwiches

and I'm back to your stories
of each thing you did without,
your voice taut and spinning
like the spokes of the wheels
on the bike you rode
to deliver those papers,
each throw poised and perfect
as one arced moment of dawn.

3

Still, not enough, you said,
to pay for the piano lessons
of a pipe welder's son,
and you carried that with you,
the hard work, the losses ripening
like fruit on top branches.
Later, when a tenor voice blossomed
in your throat like one of those miraculous
cactus flowers in your New Mexico desert
and a college offered money
for even poor boys to sing, you missed classes,
overslept, your gift weighing like the burden
of one last chance. You left and all those years
later, I never heard you sing.

Now watching this man in the check-out line
let go of his losses, I want to tell you
and myself how the surprise of an empty
wallet might be no more than one night's
clouded dream. He leaves the clerk mired
in discarded tapes, and shoulders what remains.

TWO NIGHTS

for my brother

The night you said
I don't know you anymore,
I don't know who you are,
I wondered
who taught you to say things
like that.
There in the porchlight
with your hair uncombed,
your face tense as a kite,
I wanted to say,
I am happy

though I knew you would wonder
how it was possible
after that night years ago
when you sat on the porch
with your head in your hands
and wept, the shouts in your ears
like panicked birds,
father's anger more real
than the darkened windows
of the houses across the street
or the billboards rising like giant balloons
from the highway.
I watched you from the window of the car,

just touching the outline of your body
in the glass.

Those years you decided
to build solar heaters,
to insulate houses,
to open workshops
where people came
to watch you handle the tools,
the latches, the long planes of board.
You taught them to take the hammers and nails
in their own hands, to fashion that wood
for themselves.
I dreamed of houses
roofed with glass, prayer plants
opening their leaves, the sun
every morning like a washed face,
generous, asking nothing.

When you think you don't know me,
try to remember the German village
where we caught salamanders
shiny as coins, found a porcupine
pursed in its quills.
Wolfgang and Edith led us to mushrooms
that we cooked in the woods
and later mother was frightened
to hear where we'd been, the smoke of the fire
deep in our clothes, our smiles dreamy.
That was the summer I loved the Italian,

though I told no one. When I threw the baton
high in the air and it fell to a dent
on Lucille's Corvair, it was for him.

Later Edith showed us the rabbits
fat in their cages
and I never told you
that they were for eating,
though we ate together the sweet peas
raw from her garden and the hard disks
of bread that came in the back of the truck
each Saturday, bread so animated with grains
and crust that later, back in the States,
you asked for bread, real bread,
when Lois bought the Sunbeam, each slice
insubstantial as our lives
in the houses of relatives.

That night in the porchlight
as we stood together, it was the absence
of tears, the air whole and untorn
by raised voices
that you did not recognize. It was me
smiling, outside a house that I could re-enter.
It was you, leaving, this time
without fear.

WHEN THE BLEEDING COMES

It's short. Two days of ebb
and flow. That thick swim
the first day, when pain
rifles its hot head,
I refuse the easy bliss of codeine.
It's something I need to feel,
this fiery sun at my body's horizon,
setting. The second day, I float,
intangible as flame.
Hurt only crescents me now.
It's like the abundance
of brilliant fish in a clear pool.

As sentimental as anyone's sunset snapshot,
this hankering after strollers. I know it.
But how finally to explain that frantic grief
burning over me like a brush fire.
I walk out of those cinders alone,
no hard ache of a child
to bear me back again.

THE DAUGHTER

Your father
round-headed
in overalls
cried the day his hammer hit your thumb
and not the nail
you held.
He worked no more that day,
but rocked you
on the side porch,
holding ice cubes in a towel,
coaxing your delicate fingers
in among them.
By evening you curled at his chest and slept,
new as the sprouts in his fields.
He watched
as starlings rose and fell
among the rows
planted a month ago,
just turning green.

SYCAMORE

We could not predict
its eventual size,
leaves broad as faces,
limbs the length of the lawn
leisurely reaching, rising
above the rows of roofs.

Planting it, my father cursed
the cracked red clay, struck
and scraped, a suburban Cain
forcing from earth
what she yields, only slowly.
I mixed in peat, manure.
Somehow the roots took hold,

branches large as thighs
grew, held my weight.
Loving my father more, I
knew him less. In autumn
we gathered leaves like burdens.

Winter, I watched the moon
rise from the lap of a limb
and leave alone in the night.
In this season, too,
my father died.

Now, mingling branches
with telephone wires,
boldly splitting
its improbable skin,
like a child who, lacking love,
imagines it, the sycamore
makes this yard its own.

FLIGHT

You said yourself
it was somehow right:
the cockatiel flew
on her yellow wings.
You opened the door
and she flew at an angle of light,
flew through air like a hoop.

You tell me
you left the cage
on the porch
as if she'd return
to that place
though for years
she'd prepared for flight,
dreamed of it, head
tucked under one wing.

In winter, you say
she'll freeze to the rim
of the sky. In summer
crack her beak
on the sun's rays.
But when I see her
in my dreams
she is building a nest
of brambles and down.
She is preening
a golden wing.

GROPING FOR TROUT

In a space before belief I stayed for months,
the alarm of my pregnant belly like sudden danger
in a dream.

> When your father dies behind your back, slides
> down the door of the hall closet and calls
> for no one, you expect a message in the arms
> of every man you meet, the echo of a warning.
> You remember groping for trout, bare-handed,
> in a river near Zugspitze mountain, those fins
> grazing your ankles, a splash chilling
> your thighs, then fingers spread in the empty
> water, palms turning upward in disbelief.
> You imagine tomorrow he returns from a long
> fishing trip, his catch strung up by the gills,
> then lying silver in the sink, and him tipping
> the hanger of a fresh shirt, filling an empty sleeve.

In the story, the mother of Merlin dreamed herself
a lover, lay in the arms of a half-spirit, woke
from conception without memory. Sometimes, early
morning, I remember a man after dark, that long
walk alone, then squeezing my eyes shut in the grass
beside the stream of a city park.

> Father and I kept minnows in a bucket,
> each day skimming the dead from the surface,

finally taking the survivors down to the creek.
He said they would grow to parent carp.

Child, you were a secret keeping itself. I waited
for your birth like a girl in line baring her arm
for vaccination, then bravely pulling down the sleeve,
palm cupping the elbow. Years from now when you
come home with that sore shoulder, I'll tell you how
the body teethes on its pain, makes its own cradle,
rises from its night of disease
and is well again.

SACRAMENT OF SLEEP

Like a gift, the dream arcs
through sleep, like a promise:
we may yet know ourselves.

Now while mind and body cleave
the secrets are recounted
how, loving too much or too little

the rhythm of our days shifted:
The daughter, denied, knotted
her hair and left her home.

The father dies before
his fruit trees blossom.
Perhaps, like a damaged vein,

pain, years old, collapses
forgets its source
dissolves.

The dream recalls what's lost,
offers the other selves
the other choices

from another darkness, brimming
wakes body and blood.

NOTES TO MY FATHER
THREE YEARS AFTER HIS DEATH

1

We gave the undertakers a real suit.
They wanted to lay you out like a fluke,
back bare in the coffin.
Later I dreamed I covered your eyes
with half-dollars, passage across a dark river.
I fashioned a taper the length of your body,
wound it round like a small wax pie
light enough for your journey.

2

Driving to Galveston, you stopped by the side
of the road, let the headlights of a funeral
wind past: *When I kick the bucket*
I want a pine box. That's all.
Still we bought you a regular coffin.
In the room of open lids, I imagined
shells in the shallows of the gulf.

3

Some days I tell myself the truth:
you died while I slept in another city.
No confessions, no absolutions.

4

In Romania they drive stakes through the hearts
of the restless dead. Villagers make moonshine
from plums, then dig by the light of the moon
for fathers, daughters with fists full of hair.
I think of Hamlet, that legacy of ghosts
before dawn. Or Huck, whose father mistook him
for the Angel of Death.
I watch from the window of the limousine,
see those gravediggers, their mechanical shovel
stalking your coffin.

DREAMS OF DEPARTURE

1

When she comes to this place,
she knows she's been here before:
the house of polished wood,
staircases she's climbed
a thousand times, rooms
she doesn't need to re-enter.
Even the light through the hall windows
falls in familiar patterns:
she steps into a bright square,
hesitates, and goes on.
At the end of the passage
there's a room full of women
sitting in straight-backed chairs.
Only one looks up as she enters.
This woman has something for her:
cheese and hard bread
wrapped in a cloth,
thread, a knife, a comb.
The dreamer is leaving this place,
the marbled light, the still mantles.
The woman knows:
she puts her hand in the fire
and brings out a key
from the coals.

2

She's back in the forest
again. The trees grow
thickly. Roots tangle
at her feet. She's stood here
before, the cold
settling into her clothes.
There is less fear
this time – that is
the only difference.
The darkness still
folds in.

2.   KEEPING THE FEAST

TO FEAR DEATH BY WATER

My brother told me the story: a man trapped
below a river, a logger with legs crushed
between timber. *His* brother brings air from above
the surface: dives, presses lip to lip, returns
for more. My brother says, "Here is an act
of will; here is a bond of blood." Just the same,
the trapped logger dies.

In my dreams there is water to fear: a still black lake
where knobs of cypress roots rise like bony knees,
as if bodies lay buried with legs drawn up and skulls
beneath the earth, beneath the black water.
Suddenly my brother on the edge of a diving board
above the black surface, dressed in the black suit
of divers, eyes enclosed in that clear
ellipse. I watch and am afraid. There is the question
of depth, the horror of never rising. There is the horror
of ever rising.

I ask, "Did the trapped man refuse his brother's breath?
Did he hold the borrowed air inside his cheeks and blow
into the black water before it reached his lungs?
Perhaps, like a man alone in a room for months, the act
of breathing, the fact of air, became unreal. He confuses
water with life; he opens his mouth to gulp it. Is there
ever an instant, just before dying, when he knows
he is wrong?"

My brother answers, "Imagine the air above the surface
of the river, each time the brother rising toward
enormous sky, each time filling his own lungs,
then diving to fill the lungs of his trapped
brother. Imagine, finally, the gaping mouth,
the hair waving across dead eyes,
the last rise to the surface
alone."

THE SEVENTH DAY OF CREATION

from Escher's woodcut

Eve, I have watched you long enough
to lean against the trunk of that black tree myself.
I have stood where you stand, bending my head
to gaze at him while two strands of hair fall and fork
between my breasts, while the rivers fork through
the valleys and a tongue forks in my ear.
The snake has grown the legs of a lizard
and black and white scales. The apples on the tree
hang white against the trunk and black against the sky.
My lover sits, forehead pressed in palm,
as if he is worried. His hair is as gray as the apple
turned when I picked it. Or perhaps I didn't.
Perhaps I only caught it as it fell, overripe,
from a black branch. He does not listen to this.
I watch the elephant on the opposite shore.
The grey trunk falls between tusks long as branches
into the cool river water.

BRITOMART WRITES FROM MALECASTA'S CASTLE

from Book III, The Faerie Queene

Dear Father,

Four years now I'm looking for the face
I saw in your mirror. Merlin says
I will found nations, prophesies a race
of kings. Destiny arranges my days
like seasons. At night I sing the old lais
and wonder how your life would be
had you sons, or a daughter less
strong than I am. Sometimes by means of memory
I imagine myself in my own country.

Always I win many battles, holding
the sword as you taught me
(even in dreams the metal ringing).
I recall the sins – pride, greed, jealousy –
the companions of heirs, you said. Being
so chaste, I am often alone. Now a stranger
calls me beautiful and I find myself smiling.
Tonight I will sleep without armor,
expecting no danger.

NOBEL PHYSICIST CREATES THEORY
FROM GEOLOGIST SON'S DATA

Carrying the chip of stone –
curious sediment sandwiched
by layers of lime –
you come home from Italy,
my son, without wonder.
A line of cosmic dust
separates Cretaceous
(I discover)
and Paleocene
as if with a stubby pencil
a god capricious, angry or bored
drew
    a shade across the sun,
in a fit of temper
split the earth's seam,
threw a meteor
the size of a country; by god,
a wound like that
and the sky wept ashes
three years, maybe five,
dinosaurs dropped like flies,
a whole world dies
as you my Gulliver son
tend facts and stones
in a region where
volcanoes never blister night,
continents never rise
filling empty oceans.

MAGDALENE

1

Baskets full of water,
full of wind. I carried them

through Magdala and asked
the fishermen to bend

and sort through waves,
through air. Each day

my demons drove me
to the sea, to gather

what I could not hope
to hold. My hair

pitched like the waves.
At Galilee, I thought

the shores would breach,
the sky divide and empty:

earth would throw us fiery
to its center. I could not speak

but tried to hoard in baskets
the water and the air.

2

The candle's flame
is a feather
dancing a skull,
a little plume of light.

My hand rests here
at the eye sockets.
It's as if I'd make them blink.

Tonight for the first time
when I look in the mirror,
I know I will die.

From the darkness
words arrive like lovers –
you who are without sin

3

How was it
I came to shut his words out?

His parables were stones
I wanted to throw in the lake,
create my own circle
again and again.

I want to see *my* face
reflected there,
not his, feel *my* words
rising like doves
from the water's rim.

KEEPING THE FEAST

Last Thursday was bitter
like the inside husk
shadowing a pecan. Unaware,
she took it in.
Friday tasted better,
though hours
sat on the plate,
growing cold.
She ate Saturday whole,
then Sunday in sections
like a navel orange.
By Monday his dark eyes
famish her again.
She decides to eat the week
like chocolates, slowly,
while no one is looking.

RELIVING THE MYTHS

When you see his face,
abstracted
(he's thinking of
something else),
and the feeling
rises until
you are Calypso
who would
shatter his ship,
spin a cave
around him
seven years,
keep him there
beside you
(you are so
beautiful, you say,
why not?) –

remember this:
he'll weep
every
single
day
out on the rocks.

It's like turning
from grief

to grief
to watch him
lash the logs
of that raft,
but I propose this:
that you build
a raft of your own.
In the sea air,
the waves turning
over
and over,
the body lets go
of its darkness,
retrieves it,
lets go.

You always have this:
how no one will need
to bind you
when the Sirens sing
because you know
the song
already so well,
could sing it
yourself
if you wanted.

SIGUNE TO PARZIVAL:
A DISCOURSE ON GRIEF

1

The sight of me, fists full of braids, scalp
full of blood, is the first test of heroes:
I tell you your legacy and your future,
then point you in the wrong direction.
Notice as I stretch my arm and whisper, "That way,"
the long strands of hair hanging from my fingers.
Observe the body of this man, newly dead, in my lap.
Now that he is dead, I love him.

                                    I am not a woman
who can afford another mistake, but you need advice:
Recall when you were a boy, you whittled a bow
and arrows. You carved at the white ash for days
with so little idea of what you were making.
Then turning that slender arc in your palms
you understood

                   there were birds you meant to kill.
But whenever you shot the bird whose song was so loud
before, you wept and tore your hair. Your hands
among the arrows, then your hands full of hair.
Walking to bathe your scalp in a spring

                            you wept
at the songs of birds.

Understand. It was necessary to scoop out his heart,
lungs, liver, kidneys. I remember the ropes of intestine,
how I found myself winding my hair all around them.
That night I lay down like Medusa, plaited
to dead bowels. See, I have brought my lover up
among the linden branches. Now this leaf
can be his heart. The skin of my head puckers
like a lime. I seem to wait for the sleeve of some man
casually to polish my skull.

                       Cousin, you only come to me
with failure. You turn to mirrors for comfort, as if
reflection alone could save you.
For you my mouth is wide with warnings:
Grave harm can befall a stranger here. Turn back
if life is dear to you.

                Still, I can tell you how to mend
the sword at your side when it shatters. Go to the spring
named Lac. Before dawn, catch the water at its source,
beneath the rock. If you save each splinter of iron
this water can make the thing whole again.

                         You say
I speak like a woman who does not believe her words.
You say: let us bury this dead man.

3

I live in this thatched hut, surrounded by fallen
trees. I built it from the inside, over the source
of the spring, and lived for days without windows
or doors. One morning I woke and found

                                        branches
piercing each wall, heavy with fruit.
I filled his coffin with ripe apricots, plums
in the eye sockets, a melon at his belly,
one clump of grapes between the bones of his thighs.
Here within I am not alone. He is the one and I
am the other.

                 Always you ask me the direction to take,
but I tell you my voice is ruined with lamentation.
Lately I dream of my mother,

                              how she died at my birth.
My father slipped the bark from the linden branch
and sucked and sucked at all that blood in her belly,
so much blood he could have drowned me in it.

Once you spoke with a voice you did not believe
was your own. Every sound seemed a great risk.
But I know you for a man who sees the face
of the woman he loves in three drops of blood
on the snow. Your hair sprouts thick with suffering.

Do not come to me with any more questions.

4

To sweet Herzeloyde's child:
tonight I make an embrace of bones.
It is an easy thing to pull down
the lid of this coffin.
I will take his ten fingers and
plunge them into my breasts
(up to his knuckles in flesh).
I will fill my ears with his teeth,
my crotch with the bones of his toes.

Do not grieve when you find me so.
Remember the dead Medusa:
winged horses rose from her blood.

3. WINDOW ON SPAIN

THE TRAVELER

You were always alone,
they said, with your books.
They imagined you nursing
a glass of whiskey
at midnight
with only Hume
beside you, or Kant.
Of course you knew
Foucault, what else
was there for you to do
but speak with the dead?
They invited you to dinner,
asked you to recite Pound
over grilled pork chops.
You described the stones
of Venice, and later they spoke
of your loneliness,
and their own normal lives.
And now when you bring
this woman, sit close to her
on their chintz couch
lacing your fingers
through hers, the two of you
speaking of Paris, Istanbul,
they are troubled.
They had thought they understood
the price you paid

for the lilt in your voice,
your stories. Who'd have thought
you'd appear like that
with your own life?

EL MERCADO

Just off a narrow side street,
past the bread vendors,
is the market:
hogs with enormous white haunches
stretched out on tables,
rabbits, skinned and wide-eyed,
chickens on their backs all in a row,
their yellow claws drawn up–
everything so newly slaughtered
you might reach in the air
and catch an animal's very last breath.
The fruitstands swell with another abundance:
mandarins cluster like bright orange beads,
dusty muscatel grapes smell illicit.
Here too the potatoes just as they come,
sandy and firm, and celery,
stalks broad as wrists.
One vender arranges pig's heads
on his counter. They gaze out sleepy and grinning
and he grins sleepily too,
his elbows on vacant glass.
A woman props a cow's head
in a bucket of ice – it stares up,
asking 900 pesetas.
Next aisle there's a man
surrounded by hundreds of eggs.
¿Que quieres? he says through the cartons.

His eyes have grown milky
and he moves through his stall
with something like reverence.
When he fills the bag and holds it out,
I accept it like a gift,
even imitate his movements
as I walk, slowly, away.
And when a hooded man nudges past
with a sow slung over his shoulder,
I hardly notice.
I keep holding that bag like a charm.

GOOD FRIDAY IN LOGROÑO

I could say it was like
the heartbeat of god,
but it wasn't –
it was only boys beating drums
through the narrow street
of Marques de san Nicolas,
and I was so close
I saw one stop to examine a blister.
It's true, I felt the sound
like the beat of a heart
larger than mine,
watched the others lean toward it
as I leaned away, thought:
they have felt this before.
They have seen these robes,
purple and black, red and gold,
and domed hats swaying in the night air
just lit with lanterns, swaying,
and with lights on the ends of sticks.
An old woman lifts a small boy
toward Jesus in a glass casket,
says, *¡Que bonito!* Recalling it,
I am between what I saw there in the street
and what I might tell you.
Another woman walked barefoot in a black veil,
her arms spread on a cross she imagined:
this is true – I wanted to know her sins,

how they compared with my own.
Men in green hoods and white robes
were dragging great crosses –
I tried to guess the weight,
but I think they were balsa,
the men moved so quickly.
I want to tell you someone sang a *saeta*,
how it pulsed and became a living thing,
and we each touched it and were made whole.
But instead I say Logroño's civic band
put their lips to trombone and trumpet
and played slightly off-key.
I am here now in this unbending moment,
a Protestant in Catholic Spain,
where no one gave themselves up to song
in the streets of Logroño on Good Friday,
none spoke with their soul
at the gates of their lips
or called to the Virgin like a lover.
But even this is not so. I begin again:
when the drums beat
I felt sound knock at my chest
and for a moment was a child
listening to the heartbeat of God.

AÑO NUEVO

Rosie is counting the grapes
one for each month –
if we eat them all
as the clock strikes twelve,
she says the new year will be lucky.
Buena suerte. One for each bell.
Not too quickly.
Santos sleeps off his wine
in an old lounge chair.
Beneath his black Basque beret
his face is abrupt and massive,
as if it took its cue
from the mountain cliffs of Viguera,
the pueblo where he was born.
In their kitchen, the coal stove
toasting our backs, we forget
that it's winter, though Rosie says
in thirty years it's never been this cold,
no, not like this, with the sheets
freezing on the line. She spreads
the table with dried fruit and turron,
hands around the strong coffee,
then climbs the ladder to the top shelf
for the peaches she's canned.
When she led us up the rickety stairs
to her flat, she said,
Es vieja, pero no importa.

This is the wrong side of the Rio Ebro,
but in Rosie's kitchen
the dog eats marzipan
and Santos pours dark Rioja wine.
Now when the clock strikes twelve,
we eat the grapes one by one
and we take in the bright kitchen
with them, and Santos' thick voice
and Rosie's hand on the telephone
dialing nine brothers and sisters
in Burgos, Bilbao, Victoria,
all those lives that keep going on.

CORRIDA

When she dreams a bull,
it's a dappled one –
she can just see his flanks
through the darkness.
He canters up
in a mock charge,
cunning, tossing his horns.
(She smiles at this, though she knows
she could die in an instant.)
Then, in through the door of her house
he goes, to settle on the rug,
forelegs tucked neatly under.
A crowd gathers.
Someone does the flamenco.
Now she's a matador wooing the bull
with an old beach towel,
prodding his neck with a broom.
Picadors arrive in bathrobes.
The landlord trots in on a plunger.
But beneath his wily horns,
the bull stays rooted.
Just before she wakes,
she's arranging the furniture
around him, hanging hats
from his horns.
Perhaps, she thinks,
she can live like this,
just skirting the danger.

FOR JOHN IN MADRID, 1985

He chooses me
with a question:
Are you American?
and though I expect
the half sneer
that accuses me
of missiles and money,
I say *yes*
wait
for what doesn't
come, this time
not this time anything
about bombs and bases
and how Europe
can defend itself.
Instead
he bridges us
simply:
I want to come
to your country.

He is John
from Angola
and here on Grand Via
in Madrid
over hamburgers
he tells me his story:

how the army came.
He learned Russian.
And later
he returned home
from Cuba
to find his father
dead, his mother
lost and walked
his whole country
looking.

They wanted
to kill me too.
And when I ask who:
the Communists.
I say nothing,
half-wish
it was *they*,
fascist right
with American guns.

I am ready
there
with the sun
at my back
to say:
We are wrong. We Americans,
we are misguided.

But that is not
what his story says,
this time.
In broken English,
he speaks from
a place I can't see,
deeper than
parties or factions,
from somewhere in the earth
where rock slides rock
he speaks, from a heart
fed by underground streams,
he speaks about the oil,
the diamonds they're taking,
the shops without food,
how he took the boat
to Portugal
where he could not stay
and now in Madrid
lives each month
on 22,000 pesetas
and waits for the visa,
to hear from the friend
in San Francisco.
He floats the word
asylum
like a boat that might reach
me, though I've made the waters
rough with theory
and the pride not to admit:

someone else can do wrong,
not just my country.

He will work he says
will study, will wait
for Angola
to outgrow its illness.
He says it slowly and perfectly,
what I cannot say without pain:
that he loves his country,
that he wants to go back there.

WINDOW ON SPAIN

Just outside, the laundry
I've learned to string on a pulley
joins the conversation of colors
outside other windows –
what we wore yesterday,
what we will wear tomorrow.
Down below, the landlord
pours goat's milk from a bucket
and kittens fall in
licking the milky sides –
four in October
tangling their gray stripes,
but by spring
only the mother
remains, mewing for scraps.

(Nothing orders all this
but change, how in winter
a shirt will freeze
stiff, break in half.
And the kittens,
I've told you,
disappear.)

Farther on
there's a playground,
dull gray when I came,

but men in blue jumpsuits
appeared one day, painted
it green and red and blue,
the swings swaying there
now brightly
in the morning light.

I see Julio
who runs the bar down the street
pushing his granddaughter
up and down on a see-saw,
her hair floating up like a sail.
I *saw* Julio there in October, November,
each Sunday through all the coldest months
he was there, until spring
when the stroke shut him down
and they turned off the lights in his bar.

If I look down to the left
I see large molds for tombstones.
No one ever works here
but the granite keeps finding its shape,
thick tablets, waiting.

Farther on
the shouts of young boys playing soccer–
a thicket of legs
racing the ball down the field,
the field lined with the wall
of a graveyard.

Now the boys running.
Now the walls they run past.

Looking up
I see brown mountains
shouldering the sky.

From all that I've seen
I choose this:
a man with a cart
piling fresh grass,
bending here and there
to scythe it,
finally gathering the piles
high in his cart
and placing his children on top.
Off they go, through the playground,
the man leading the donkey.
Through the soccer field,
the children diving
into the fresh load of grass.
Past the graveyard,
the cart leaving
bright swatches of green.

They do not stop.
They go on from their green trail.

4. LIVING TOGETHER

A POET EXPLAINS DECONSTRUCTION

what is this but words
come home like pigeons
sent out with a message
you cannot remember

you have only their fast shadows
in afternoon light
their feet unburdened
they bring no reply

you expect something
cryptic
a riddle
about wings and light and air
you might answer
and this day become a kingdom
you might stand like a statue
at its center

instead you pull curtains past glass
these birds might mistake
for a portion of air
let them play
you say
let them
careen the light

LIVING TOGETHER

Old Mrs. Slatterfield paces her yard
in a pink bathrobe. She is all stomach
and frown. She looks like a dyed Easter chick,
pointing her toes in slick, shiny grass.
Some days she is more like a barge,
poling the boat of her body
across the low tide of her porch,
then setting sail in a paisley house dress
for the mailbox at the side of the road.
I watch her because she is there
living alone with her middle-aged son.
They sit on the porch in the evenings
courting the breeze, smoking cigarettes,
their voices filtering the darkness
like stirred leaves.
I watch her because she watches me,
living alone in this house with my lover.
Perhaps she's displeased by the untended yard,
the kudzu curling the posts of my porch.
In two years
she only calls to me once:
You the same girl been living there
all this time?

I might have given her a bowl
of wild roses, dried petals
for a sachet to scent her clothes.

She might have taught me
pie crust, a way of pruning shrubs.
Instead we are outlaws
in our own neighborhood
and in our hearts
because we have what we wanted.
When she heads for Ingles in her gold Malibu,
we both look toward the Baptist Church
on the corner, and do not wave.

ON LAUNDRY

To find pleasure in this –

wind puffing the sleeves of shirts,
as if spirits sought, momentarily,
to clothe themselves, socks flapping
like flags, the whole line beckoning,
halting, teasing the wet into air –

is simply unlike myself.
                              I abandon

the hot whirl of machines, the spiral
of front load, for water in a bucket
and soap between my fingers.

I discover a litany of touch:
the cascade from the faucet,
my chill wrist beneath cotton
translucent as a second skin.

Here is blood, staining a crotch.
I smile at the bloom in white linen
after all these careful years.

Sometimes his denim drinks so deeply
trousers fill a bucket alone.
I spill them into the basin, watch

the tile tinge blue and know
this is not loss.
                  On the line
sheets poise on their corners,
dance in the afternoon heat.
Light billows light.

HOLDING TIGHT

for Luke

I still see you sometimes in crowds.
You are there among all the others
I had not meant to lose,
tall, your hair just thinning.
In an airport, a man in a beige jacket
with your jaunty smile reminds me
of that May afternoon, heavy with rain,
when we stood inside the glass doors
saying our goodbyes. We spoke of a visit
I might make to the coast
and I took the edge off our parting
by hurrying off to a lecture.

When you tested HIV positive,
it wasn't only me you never told.
I remember you at my dinner table,
fastidious, hardly touching the food,
your hand on my arm as I reached
for a taste of your wine.
You protected us all from your danger,
knowing, perhaps, we'd have shown no mercy,
shrouded you early in grief.
Don't hold so tight to life, you once told me.
When I heard the news and reached for the phone,
thinking there was time yet between us,
you were long past speaking.

At the funeral I wanted to tell the story:
how you left that village in Newfoundland
where you taught school years ago.
The priest was afraid you might fondle his boys.
He waited with your bags at the bottom of the stairs
while the landlady wept into her apron.
For a moment you looked out at the sea
and thought of each child with whom you were parting.
The tide had come in. Your face in the mirror
was the color of sand. That was how, you said,
you learned the value of secrets.

But we all taught you to keep them:
your Catholic mother with her daily confession,
your father at the piano weeping over his music,
your friends refusing to ask the right question.

SHARK'S TEETH

Even at the beach she wore her beehive hairdo,
lacquered stiff as a helmet,
only a few wisps of hair at the front
allowed to move.
I was young then and I laughed at the hours
she spent, inching down the shoreline,
her shoulders scalding red,
her size four body so top-heavy with hair,
the wind might have blown her over
and anchored her in the surf.
And always, her eyes clasped to the sand
looking for shark's teeth.

She found them by the dozen,
lined them in her palm each evening
like tiny stilettos – sand shark, bull and mako
while in the next room
I took her only son in my arms
and tried for years to love him.
He wore a dark tooth on a chain.
Perhaps she thought a relic
from something that fierce
would protect him.

Back home in the ranch house
she'd open the base of a glass lamp
to thousands of fossilized teeth,

add the newest, curved and sharp,
sprinkling them carefully
like the final ingredient of a complex spell.

And it was a spell that held me,
lifting its snout, arching its back,
dropping its pectoral fins,
took me in its jaws and asked me
to give up my life
as she had, marriage
like a shipwreck, talents
lost or buried, each day
a long surrender
to the dark glamour of loss.

Mother-in-law, from another life,
last summer I walked my own shoreline
and found (or it found me)
the gleaming tooth of a dusky shark.
I picked it up and forgave you
as perhaps you have forgiven me.

TEMPERANCE

I am walking
a ribbon of water.
Irises flame at the shore.
To balance like this
I need wings.
I spread them, just so
and hover, the sun
at my throat.
I would speak to you
of this, but you know it:
how we rise
from that dark pool
into this stunning light,
how our paths
divide the mountains
and we hold our lives
like chalices, gently.

THE QUARREL

When you bought the Christmas tree
our quarrel made you take
the one with roots, burlap-wrapped,
heavier than the two of us
could ever lift.

Seeing it wedged in the hatchback,
I knew the sure deft blow
of what you'd said
was taken back
like the awkward jerks
of a film reversed, the palm
springing back from the face it slapped,
the cheek growing pale before the sting.

We strained to land it on the cart
you use for changing oil,
the solid frozen roots, the live branches,
then rushed along the walk,
needled, thrown off, a wild zigzag
toward the door where we're faced
with a hundred pounds or more
to lift across the threshold
like an unwieldy bride.

And it's pushed, hauled, shoved inside
to the spectacle of clean intended space

on the glass-topped end table.
Whose plan was this? you asked.
Already I see us hours on,
defeated by sheer weight, by lack
of space, sawing.

I rolled the root ball
like a severed head
across the parking lot.
Criminal, I looked both ways
then pushed the heap
over the gully's lip.
I'm sure it lies there still.

I like to think the roots worked free.
Sprigs greened the stump
and the tree grew back like love.
But I never looked to see.

CLAIMING GRACE

He's back on my doorstep
By the grace of god, sister
his body caved-in, his voice
laced with hunger

*I used to work down the road
Jesus have mercy*

until I'm thrusting dollar bills
out the screen door, afraid
he'll stay like every heartache
I've ever known, claim me.

When I speak of him to friends,
they lower their eyes,
warn me to keep the door closed.
I don't say I've thought
of asking him in.

By the grace of god, sister

But the next time
after handing out oranges, grapes
I let the screen slam shut,
lattice our faces, say
This is the last time.

If he knocks again,
I'll pretend he's not out there,
retreat to the back room,
Jesus have mercy
sit stony in an armchair,
lacing my fingers.

WAITING FOR THE TRAIN

A woman runs in through smudged glass doors
chased by a man in a purple suit.
Too drunk for sharp turns, the man
falls to his knees. The woman
gains time, clatters past the passengers,
leaves a black and white shoe

stranded in the aisle. We eye the shoe,
white passengers seated rigid near the glass doors,
and toward the platforms, the black passengers.
Now the man in the purple suit
is up, yelling something slurred at the woman.
She screams, then changes pitch, laughs at the man.

From the Amtrak office, a stout man
in a tie emerges, steps between them. He scuffs his shoe
on the gray linoleum. The woman,
distracted, backs through the platform doors,
disappears. The man in the purple suit,
eyes half-mast, veers toward the rows of passengers,

then staggers after her. The faces of the white passengers
flush with relief. In a hushed, quick voice a man
in a windbreaker speaks to a woman in a gray suit.
Their eyes move from the black and white shoe
in the aisle to the slow swinging of the platform doors.
This is the violence she expected, says the woman

here in a dark city after midnight. Another woman
turns to her neighbor in the row of black passengers,
nods toward the swinging platform doors.
She says she knows the family of the man
in the purple suit, knows the woman who lost her shoe.
It's clear they don't suit.

She shakes her head and others follow suit,
their voices calm as they speak of the woman
and point, smiling, at the stranded shoe.
From the office, an announcement for the passengers:
Entertainment arranged by Amtrak, says the man
in the tie, to pass the slow hours. The platform doors

creak open and, awaiting the final scene, the passengers
turn to watch the woman retrieve her shoe. The man
in the purple suit bows, exits through the smudged doors.

MAIN STREET, MIDNIGHT AFTER RAIN

A taxi drags its wide tail
like a duck
then with a thick splash
is gone. The street
hums to itself
tunes the rain brought to mind.
Two trees drip a delicious sweat
as if after love.
One arches into the blue night.
The other bends toward grass and pavement
relaxing now, speaking of old friends.
The men are gone from the Phillips 66,
but the telephone rings on
like the call of a mother,
not insistent, giving in easily
to another hour. The one-way sign
blinks lazily into headlights
and sleeps again.

INTERSTATE 75

Just the thought of it
makes her heart beat faster:
lanes multiplying like lies,
exit ramps swirling over her head,
billboards startling as omens.
And everywhere the sinister innocence
of speed. Cars flash by
and their drivers look comfortable
as if they are sitting on sofas
after Sunday dinner.
She wants to catch their ease
like a cold, believe, like them
there's nothing to this.

Instead she dreams of mass transit,
the capable bulk of buses,
subways gliding from stop to stop,
a book on her lap, parcels
stowed at her feet like treasure.
She suspects it's unAmerican, really,
not to love this headlong motion,
this freedom (so the car ads say).

She'd take to the asphalt
with a pick ax (who on earth needs
16 lanes?), haul in topsoil,
plant grasses and wildflowers,

pitch brilliant carnival tents
where lovers spread picnics,
sip wine, give way to sleep
their heads in one another's laps,
the air spiced and sweet.

But for now she drives doggedly on,
straight-backed and pokey,
hugging the side of the road,
mantras on her lips and *oh god*
her heart coaxed to steadiness
by the rise and fall of deep breathing.

HYPOGLYCEMIA

The slow razzle
of wavering blood
after, I don't know,
too many grapes

and I'm back to my body
pitching like a jonboat.

Grapes have the highest sugar content
of any fruit –
that's the kind of information
I'm full of, though it doesn't stop
me pretending
the body's loose struts
are something imagined
like the dark thought at 2 A.M.
washed away by morning light.

Perhaps it's the infant
I've not yet had
clamoring for the regular feeding
of sound, nourishing food,

or maybe the fiery teenager
I've not yet outgrown,
fond of the dinner table brawl,
embracing some needed restraint.

But I prefer this:
it's a gift
which after a sensible meal
makes a ripe apricot
stunning, a single banana
pure rapture and mangos
ecstasy.

WHAT I KNEW

1

Maybe hands touching
on the back seat of a car,
once. Or the boy
with the pointed shoes
when I was twelve.
We picked mushrooms.
He carried me across
a stream
and I made a fire
where we cooked them.
That was something like desire,
that taste, the smoke curling
our hands, our heads bent
and the air so still.

For years after that
those bodies next to mine
were like a parade
I was watching.

2

When you walked up
to my picture of St. George
and the dragon,

I was already watching
the woman in the corner
with her hands clasped,
and you were watching her
too, until
she seemed to float
past George,
past the dragon,
and enter my body
like a flame
just touched to the wick
of a candle.

3

When we lit candles
and lay down to that light,
I remembered the words
I heard in the forest,
the boy with the pointed shoes:
Carita. My dear.

4

Now let me tell you my dream:

I am standing in the aisle
of a train
watching a man who sits silent.
With the toe of my shoe

I draw a circle around myself,
smile at the man
who is you.

Suddenly, at the window,
a forest, then a maypole
wreathed with purple irises,
hundreds of them,
and white lilies.
The passengers cheer,
and when I turn toward you
my arms fill with lilies.

That is what I remember.
My arms full of lilies.

THE PLEDGE

In the evenings you bend over a book,
your body whispering from a cone of lamplight
there in the room we painted and papered,
mixing a dimestore tube of tint
with the landlord's paint,
pale gray for the trim,
blue for the door.

You papered the walls to surprise me,
burgundy blooms on green stems.
When I opened the door,
I found myself in the garden you'd made.

From friends I hear the stories:
poets and their marriages,
pain arranged in perfect lines.

One sits at the dinner table
with a wife who never reads his poems.
He hoards the prizes
alone in the room upstairs.
She looks away, her body a pressed flower.

Another invites his lover home
where she lives with his wife and child.
For years his wife fears leaving the house,
though her pain grows there, sweet and poisonous.
Lately, her child's face is the only one she knows.

Sometimes you look up, read aloud from your book,
them mark the place and make tea,
mine the one with honey.
There is still the Romanian coat in your closet,
the one you bought for a lover,
though you left her before it was given
and now the closet smells of sheepskin.
And there is the home you miss,
your fears for your father
alone through each dark English winter.
Together we could cultivate these pains
into forests of poems.

Instead, I write these quieter lines
at noon, when the air is yeasty
with bread rising and the cats
shoot the bathtub stopper like a puck
across the kitchen floor.
I know that a poem can be beautiful
but, my love, so is the sound of your voice
in the darkness and so is the room
that we made for each other
where caladiums pulse on their slender stalks
and light weaves the room like a Mexican blanket.
The writer in me pledges this:
what I make here is not better than my life.